Post Play HoopHandbook

Footwork, Scoring Moves, Back-To-Basket, Facing Up, Finishing: Everything You Need

Dre Baldwin

Copyright © 2017 Work On Your Game Inc.

All rights reserved.

ISBN: 1977766315
ISBN-13: 978-1977766311

Cover Artwork: Sam Robles

DEDICATION

To You: Your purchase of this program indicates you are ready to **Work On Your Game.**

CONTENTS

DEDICATION	**iii**
CONTENTS	**iv**
The Post: Footwork, Skill And High-Percentage Scoring	1
Series #1	**6**
Day 1	6
Day 2	7
Day 3	8
Day 4	9
Day 5	10
Day 6	11
Day 7	12
Series #2	**13**
Day 1	13
Day 2	14
Day 3	15
Day 4	16
Day 5	17
Day 6	18
Day 7	19
Series #3	**20**
Day 1	20
Day 2	21
Day 3	22
Day 4	23
Day 5	24
Day 6	25
Day 7	26
Workout Tracker: 365 Days	**28**
About Dre Baldwin	**58**

Other Books By Dre Baldwin   **59**

Other HoopHandbook Programs   **60**

THE POST: FOOTWORK, SKILL AND HIGH-PERCENTAGE SCORING

As basketball evolves, more and more players are developing an all-around game. Every player wants to handle the ball, shoot three-point shots, and be effective offensively from anywhere on the floor.

That's great — at HoopHandbook, we have the materials to help you develop all of those skills and more.

The post, however, is one area that some players stay away from, hoping to avoid the stigma of being labelled a "big" player. Bigs are traditionally allowed to play touch the ball only around the basket, no dribbling and discouraged from shooting jumpshots.

As a player who was taller than most of my peers in my teen years, I completely understand.

I hated when shorter players would tell me to "go down low" only because of my height, not concerned with what I was actually capable of doing. It was even worse when coaches would pigeonhole me into playing a "big" position due to me being one of the taller players on the roster.

As I got better and went to higher levels of the game, the size factor evened out and I was not the tallest guy anymore. I could finally display the perimeter skills I'd been working on on my own.

BUT, despite the fact that I could finally play "my game" on the outside, I never shunned an opportunity to score in the post.

As a player, I always believed I should have no holes in my game. I never wanted to be a player who was really good at some areas of basketball while being a complete non-factor in others. To me, any holes in my game made me a possible liability, depending on who I was playing with and who we playing against. To be a versatile, all-around player, being able to score in the post — even if I didn't need or get to use it as much — was just as important as any other skill.

If I got one opportunity all year to score in the post and it converted into points, those points could be the difference between winning and losing a playoff game or between making and not making a team.

Would the work then be worth it? For me, absolutely. And this mindset applied to every facet of basketball.

Since you have this program, I hope your answer and mindset is the same. Any other skill you're lacking in, go to HoopHandbook.com and plug those holes.

This program covers every skill and tool you'll need to be an effective post scorer, including:

- Footwork
- Finishing at the rim
- Scoring with both hands
- Using your body
- Shooting from the post

What I require of you:

1. **Follow the program.** This program has been designed and followed by a professional player — me — and I know what I'm doing. I don't care what anyone else has told you, what your bum friends at the park say, or what you saw on YouTube two weeks ago. Follow what I tell you to do.

2. **Go hard with each repetition.** No need to pace yourself here. The program is designed to fatigue you, but no so much that you're doing "lazy" reps at the end of the workouts (unless you're in terrible shape — get Ultimate Athlete

to help you with that). Put your full effort into each rep.

Understand: Full effort is mental decision much more than a physical capability.

3. **Stick to the Disciplines.** You will do some of the same drills over and over again in this program. It's not a mistake — do it as I tell you to do it.

Repetition is the mother of skill, though it can be monotonous. Which is why most people who love playing basketball never go anywhere in basketball: They only want to do what's fun and exciting. Becoming good is boring and repetitive.

You don't get good from doing random stuff every day. Discipline is freedom.

4. **Take care of your body between workouts.** This means
    1) Water — drink plenty
    2) Stretching — this helps your muscles recover
    3) Rest — 8 hours of nightly sleep, and rest your legs as much a you can when you're awake.

Make excuses for your inability to do these if you wish; you will pay for it with less-than-ideal results.

All drill videos are here: HoopHandbook.com/PostDrills

***

Anything you need, or anything I may have missed (typos?), reach me directly at the channels below. I receive lots of messages, so be patient. Don't send the same message twice :)

Twitter @DreAllDay
Instagram @DreBaldwin
Snapchat @DreBaldwin
Facebook /WorkOnYourGame
Dre@DreAllDay.com

- Dre

SERIES #1

Day 1

1. **Mikan Drill (Watch) and Reverse Mikan Drill (Watch)** - Make **20 in a row** in both. If you miss, start over. Missing layups is unacceptable.

2. **One Hand, One Foot Bank Drill (Watch Watch)** - Position yourself 5-8 feet from the hoop at an angle. Take a small step to jump (not so high) off of one foot and shoot a bank off the glass. The purpose of this is practicing making the bank while turning and jumping off of one foot, not how high you are jumping. Make 15 on each side of the basket.

3. **Quick Baseline Drop-Step Hook Shot (Watch Watch)** - Have your back turned to the hoop. Whichever hand you are shooting with, the drop-step is done with the opposite foot (ie, shooting with your right hand, drop step with your left foot). This move is the 'layup' of post skills. Make 20 with your right hand and 20 with your left.

4. **Middle Drop Step Scoop (Watch)** - Drop your inside foot towards the middle of the lane, swooping in with the ball in the opposite hand of the drop-stepping foot. Finish on the opposite side of the rim from where the move began. Make 7 each side.

5. **Drop-Step Step-Thru Move (Watch)** - Step up the same way as the drop step move. You fake the shot and step through with the opposite foot that performed the drop step. Finish on the corresponding side of the rim. Make 15 on each side.

6. **Baseline Drop Step Up-And-Under (Watch)** - Drop step towards the baseline, and give a shot fake. With your back foot, step through towards the basket and finish at the rim. Make 12 from each side of the lane.

Day 2

1. **Mikan Drill and Reverse Mikan Drill** - Make **20 in a row** in both. If you miss, start over. Missing layups is unacceptable.

2. **Middle Drop-Step Up-And-Under Move (Watch)** - With a live back-to-basket dribble, flash a shoulder and foot towards the baseline. Step that same leg towards the middle and show ball for a shot fake, then step thru for a layup. The pivot foot must stay down throughout the move until you jump off of both feet for the finish. Make 10 each side.

3. **Running Hook Shot (Watch)** - Take one dribble from the side of the basket, two running steps, and finish your shot over the top of your body. On each side of the hoop, make 5 starting in a face-up position and also 5 from a back-to-the-basket position. 20 total makes.

4. **Face-Up One Dribble Hook Shot (Watch)** - Turn and face your defender. Take one dribble towards the middle of the floor (or to the right/left if you started in the middle), elevate and make a jump hook. Make 15 each side.

5. **Face-Up Jab Jumpstop Shot (Watch Watch)** - Catch a pass and turn to face your defender, jabbing towards the baseline. Attack in the opposite direction -- towards the middle -- with one dribble. Jumpstop and elevate for a short jumper. Make 12 each side.

Day 3

1. **Mikan Drill and Reverse Mikan Drill** - Make **20 in a row** in both. If you miss, start over. Missing layups is unacceptable.

2. **Turnaround Jumpshot (Watch)** - Flash one shoulder as a fake, drop the opposite foot and shoot your shot going in that opposite direction. Elevation on the shot is important to get a clean look. Make 8 over your left and right shoulders from both sides of the lane; 32 total makes.

3. **Power-In Post Move (Watch)** - Catching the ball with back to the basket, drop your shoulder closest to the baseline -- enough that you can touch the floor or close to it -- take one power dribble and big step to the basket, and power up for your finish. Make 12 on each side.

4. **Post Drop-Spin Move (Watch)** - After catching the ball with your back to the basket, you take advantage of a defender leaning on you. Drop the foot that is closest to the baseline next to (and outside of) your defender's foot (not in-between her feet, but outside of them). Drop the ball as your first dribble and go in and finish. You may need to use additional dribbles depending on your distance from the basket. Make 15 each side.

5. **Post Catch & Spin Move (Watch Watch)** - Here you will use a defender's resistance to your advantage. As the pass comes in to your hands, drop your foot that is closest to the baseline, plant and spin on it (the other foot is what you use to push off and create the turning momentum). Drop your closest-to-baseline shoulder, dribbling the ball with the corresponding hand, and drive to your finish (taking another dribble if you need it). Make 12 each side.

6. **Low Swing, Middle Spin (Watch)** - From the block area or further out (enough space that you can dribble towards the baseline), attack with your dribble to the baseline. Plant, pivot and spin back towards the middle/ foul line and finish. Make 8 each side.

Day 4

1. **Mikan Drill and Reverse Mikan Drill** - Make **20 in a row** in both. If you miss, start over. Missing layups is unacceptable.

2. **Face-Up Pound-Crossover Drive (Watch)** - After receiving the ball with your back to the basket, turn and face your defender. Jab step and use a low, hard pound dribble right in front of your toes on the same foot you are jabbing with. Immediately cross over dribble and drive in to finish (making this a 2-dribble move). It is very important that your pound dribble be very low, as your defender is closer to you than doing this move from the perimeter. Make 12 each side.

3. **Face-Up Jab-Crossover (Watch)** - The setup and execution of this move is the same as the previous, except there is no 'pound' dribble. You jab step, bringing the ball out in the same direction as your jab (but not dribbling it), and cross over dribble, and finish at the basket. Be careful to keep the toes of your pivot foot (the foot you didn't jab with) down as your perform the move. Make 10 each side. (You can also add a shot fake to this move -- See Here)

4. **Face-Up Explode Drive (Watch)** - Catch and face up your defender 10-15 feet away from the hoop. Jab hard towards the middle of the floor, immediately attacking in the opposite direction. You must get low and dip the shoulder of the same side you jabbed with to squeeze past a close defender. Take two steps and explode aggressively to the basket. Keep the pivot foot (toes) down on the jab. Make 12 each side.

5. **Face-Up Jab Pivot Spin Move (Watch Watch)** - This is a mis-direction combo move predicated in footwork. Jab towards the baseline, one-dribble the opposite direction, pivot and spin back towards the basket, and finish. Take the time to get the footwork correct. Make 8 each side.

Day 5

1. **Mikan Drill and Reverse Mikan Drill** - Make **20 in a row** in both. If you miss, start over. Missing layups is unacceptable.

2. **Back-To-Basket Jumpstop (Watch)** - With a live dribble and your back to your defender, plant your inside foot and jumpstop towards the middle of the floor, turning to face the hoop at the same time. Landing from the jumpstop, elevate and make your shot. 14 each side.

3. **Shot Fake Spin Up & Under (Watch)** - Turn and fake a baseline fadeaway jumper off the catch (meaning you have not dribbled yet). Still facing the basket, step thru and take one dribble. Perform a spin move towards the baseline, finishing on the other side of the rim. Footwork will make or break this move. Make 8 each side.

4. **Middle Attack Spin Move (Watch)** - Catch and face. Jab step baseline and dribble towards the middle of the lane. Perform a quick spin-hop move -- your spin move lands you on both feet -- and finish. Make 10 each side.

5. **Jab Step Low-Rip Drive (Watch)** - From the high post, rip the ball low (by the defender's ankles) and attack the basket off of one or two dribbles. If you cannot dunk this move can be finished with a short bank or hook shot. Make 14 each side.

Day 6

1. **Mikan Drill and Reverse Mikan Drill** - Make **20 in a row** in both. If you miss, start over. Missing layups is unacceptable.

2. **Baseline Turnaround Shot Fake, Middle Turnaround Jumper (Watch)** - Catch the pass and pivot towards the baseline to fake a shot (your ability to make this shot sells the fake). Begin your dribble and turn your back to your defender. Pivot on the foot furthest from the baseline, and shoot a turnaround jumpshot moving towards the foul line. Make 12 each side.

3. **Baseline Shot Fake, Middle Shot Fake Step-Thru Finish (Watch)** - Exact same as above, except for the ending: you fake the turnaround in the middle, too (so, two shot fakes), and step-thru for a leaning layup/ bank shot. Make 12 each side.

4. **Back-To Basket Jab Pivot Spin Move (Watch)** - With back turned to the basket, jab with the high-side foot (the foot furthest from the baseline) towards the foul line (head & shoulder fake also in the same direction). On the other (pivot) foot, spin to the basket while keeping your toes down, taking one dribble and finishing. Make 10 on each side.

5. **Rip-Thru Spin Step-Thru Move (Watch)** -- Explaining this in words would confuse more than it would explain. Watch the clip, and pay close attention to the footwork. Make 10 both sides.

6. **Double Spin Move (Watch)** - Immediately upon the catch, drop-spin to the baseline. Take one or two dribbles and spin right back the other direction, which should place you directly under/ in front of the basket. Finish in any way necessary. Make 6 each side.

Day 7

1. **Mikan Drill and Reverse Mikan Drill** - Make **20 in a row** in both. If you miss, start over. Missing layups is unacceptable.

2. **10 Foot Banker (Watch)** - 10-12 feet from the hoop at an angle, catch the ball with your back to the basket. Open up so that your jabbing foot is that which is closest to the baseline. Jab step once or twice, go up for your shot, off glass. Make 15 on the left and 15 on the right.

3. **Baseline Shot Fake One Dribble Drive (Watch)** - Step out to receive a pass 15 feet from the basket on the baseline. Give a shot fake and drive baseline with one or two dribbles, finishing at the rim. 12 makes on each baseline.

4. **High Post Spin Baseline Jumper (Watch Watch)** - At the elbow area with the ball and your back to the basket, spin towards and attack the baseline with one or two dribbles. Elevate and make your shot. Depending on your distance from the basket, this can be a jump hook or jumpshot. Make 12 each side.

5. **Face-Up Stepback Jumper (Watch)** - Catch the ball and immediately face up your defender. Jab right at your defender with the foot closest to the baseline, simultaneously doing a short, hard dribble with the opposite hand. Hop backwards and make your shot. Make 12 each side.

SERIES #2

Day 1

1. **Backing Down in Lane Jumpstop Finish** Get as deep as you can, with respect to your strength matchup and the help defenders. Jumpstop out of the back-down and finish from there. Try to cover significant ground with the jumpstop, even if it takes you horizontally -- an open look is what you seek.

2. **Baseline Catch - Shot Fake, Behind Back Move Finish** Start to attack the middle after your shot fake, then make a quick behind-back move to the baseline and finish.

3. **Shot Fake Baseline Pivot Step-In Shot** Raise your defender up out of her stance or off her feet with the ball fake, and step in, past her outside foot, for your shot. Do not try to avoid contact.

4. **Mid-Post Stepback Jumpshot** Face up to the defense, and use a jab step as you dribble, right into a jumper.

Day 2

1. **Quick-Pivot Right-Hand Hook Shot** Immediately upon catching the ball, plant & turn on your left foot and shoot off the glass with your right hand (switch the foot/hand on the other side).

2. **Guard Post Spin-Move Drive** With a defender leaning on your back or hip, turn with your dribble -- taking the ball around with you -- and get low to beat the defender. Get to the rim and finish.

3. **Turning & Running Hook Shot** Facing up or sideways to the defense, take one dribble and two big steps going parallel to the basket and shoot the hook up over your head.

4. **Low Block Up & Under Move** With you back to the basket, pivot and turn as in a fadeaway jumpshot. Show the ball while keeping you pivot foot down (turn on the toes), then step through with your other leg and finish.

Day 3

1. **Face-Up, Midpost Shot Fake Step-Thru Bank Shot** From the mid-post, show ball with a high shot fake, the step in -- across you other foot -- and finish off the glass.

2. **Shot Fake, One-Dribble Pivot-Spin Move Pullup Jumper** Fake the shot and use a crossover step to attack the middle of the floor. Drop your knee to a 90 degree angle, pivoting and spinning back to the baseline.

3. **Shot Fake Baseline Pivot Step-In Shot** Raise your defender up out of her stance or off her feet with the ball fake, and step in, past her outside foot, for your shot. Do not try to avoid contact.

4. **Reverse Pivot Move Layup** Maintaining your pivot foot is key here. With your back turned, swing your baseline-side leg to the middle and fake the shot. Swing that same leg back behind you, jumping and turning to adjust in the air, finishing with a layup.

Day 4

1. **Backing Down in Lane Jumpstop Finish** Get as deep as you can, with respect to your strength matchup and the help defenders. Jumpstop out of the back-down and finish from there. Try to cover significant ground with the jumpstop, even if it takes you horizontally -- an open look is what you seek.

2. **Baseline Catch - Shot Fake, Behind Back Move Finish** Start to attack the middle after your shot fake, then make a quick behind-back move to the baseline and finish.

3. **Turning & Running Hook Shot** Facing up or sideways to the defense, take one dribble and two big steps going parallel to the basket and shoot the hook up over your head.

4. **Low Block Up & Under Move** With you back to the basket, pivot and turn as in a fadeaway jumpshot. Show the ball while keeping you pivot foot down (turn on the toes), then step through with your other leg and finish.

Day 5

1. **Face-Up, Midpost Shot Fake Step-Thru Bank Shot** From the mid-post, show ball with a high shot fake, the step in -- across you other foot -- and finish off the glass.

2. **Face-Up Drive, Double Show-Ball Fake, Finish** Attack off the dribble and extend your arm out to the side with the ball in it. Bring it back in and show ball on a shit fake, then step in and finish the layup.

3. **Guard Post Spin-Move Drive** With a defender leaning on your back or hip, turn with your dribble -- taking the ball around with you -- and get low to beat the defender. Get to the rim and finish.

4. **High Post Catch, Jab & Turn Jumpshot** Upon receiving the ball, jab your inside foot towards the paint. Then, swing that same leg around you, setting your feet, and firing.

Day 6

1. **Quick-Pivot Right-Hand Hook Shot** Immediately upon catching the ball, plant & turn on your left foot and shoot off the glass with your right hand (switch the foot/hand on the other side).

2. **Shot Fake, One-Dribble Pivot-Spin Move Pullup Jumper** Fake the shot and use a crossover step to attack the middle of the floor. Drop your knee to a 90 degree angle, pivoting and spinning back to the baseline.

3. **High Post Catch, Jab & Turn Jumpshot** Upon receiving the ball, jab your inside foot towards the paint. Then, swing that same leg around you, setting your feet, and firing.

4. **Fade Away / Turn Around Jumpshot** Adjusting your touch is the key to making this shot. Your momentum is going away from the hoop so you must compensate for that. Practice will improve your accuracy.

Day 7

1. **Face-Up Drive, Double Show-Ball Fake, Finish** Attack off the dribble and extend your arm out to the side with the ball in it. Bring it back in and show ball on a shit fake, then step in and finish the layup.

2. **Mid-Post Stepback Jumpshot** Face up to the defense, and use a jab step as you dribble, right into a jumper.

3. **Reverse Pivot Move Layup** Maintaining your pivot foot is key here. With your back turned, swing your baseline-side leg to the middle and fake the shot. Swing that same leg back behind you, jumping and turning to adjust in the air, finishing with a layup.

4. **Baseline Fadeaway Jumper Counter Move - Pivot-Spin Move Finish** Work on both options for the specified reps, each. After showing you can make the fadeaway jumper, use that threat to explode to the rim.

SERIES #3

Day 1

1. **Backing Down in Lane Jumpstop Finish** Get as deep as you can, with respect to your strength matchup and the help defenders. Jumpstop out of the back-down and finish from there. Try to cover significant ground with the jumpstop, even if it takes you horizontally -- an open look is what you seek.

2. **Baseline Catch - Shot Fake, Behind Back Move Finish** Start to attack the middle after your shot fake, then make a quick behind-back move to the baseline and finish.

3. **Shot Fake Baseline Pivot Step-In Shot** Raise your defender up out of her stance or off her feet with the ball fake, and step in, past her outside foot, for your shot. Do not try to avoid contact.

4. **Mid-Post Stepback Jumpshot** Face up to the defense, and use a jab step as you dribble, right into a jumper.

Day 2

1. **Quick-Pivot Right-Hand Hook Shot** Immediately upon catching the ball, plant & turn on your left foot and shoot off the glass with your right hand (switch the foot/hand on the other side).

2. **Guard Post Spin-Move Drive** With a defender leaning on your back or hip, turn with your dribble -- taking the ball around with you -- and get low to beat the defender. Get to the rim and finish.

3. **Turning & Running Hook Shot** Facing up or sideways to the defense, take one dribble and two big steps going parallel to the basket and shoot the hook up over your head.

4. **Low Block Up & Under Move** With you back to the basket, pivot and turn as in a fadeaway jumpshot. Show the ball while keeping you pivot foot down (turn on the toes), then step through with your other leg and finish.

Day 3

1. **Face-Up, Midpost Shot Fake Step-Thru Bank Shot** From the mid-post, show ball with a high shot fake, the step in -- across you other foot -- and finish off the glass.

2. **Shot Fake, One-Dribble Pivot-Spin Move Pullup Jumper** Fake the shot and use a crossover step to attack the middle of the floor. Drop your knee to a 90 degree angle, pivoting and spinning back to the baseline.

3. **Shot Fake Baseline Pivot Step-In Shot** Raise your defender up out of her stance or off her feet with the ball fake, and step in, past her outside foot, for your shot. Do not try to avoid contact.

4. **Reverse Pivot Move Layup** Maintaining your pivot foot is key here. With your back turned, swing your baseline-side leg to the middle and fake the shot. Swing that same leg back behind you, jumping and turning to adjust in the air, finishing with a layup.

Day 4

1. **Backing Down in Lane Jumpstop Finish** Get as deep as you can, with respect to your strength matchup and the help defenders. Jumpstop out of the back-down and finish from there. Try to cover significant ground with the jumpstop, even if it takes you horizontally -- an open look is what you seek.

2. **Baseline Catch - Shot Fake, Behind Back Move Finish** Start to attack the middle after your shot fake, then make a quick behind-back move to the baseline and finish.

3. **Turning & Running Hook Shot** Facing up or sideways to the defense, take one dribble and two big steps going parallel to the basket and shoot the hook up over your head.

4. **Low Block Up & Under Move** With you back to the basket, pivot and turn as in a fadeaway jumpshot. Show the ball while keeping you pivot foot down (turn on the toes), then step through with your other leg and finish.

Day 5

1. **Face-Up, Midpost Shot Fake Step-Thru Bank Shot** From the mid-post, show ball with a high shot fake, the step in -- across you other foot -- and finish off the glass.

2. **Face-Up Drive, Double Show-Ball Fake, Finish** Attack off the dribble and extend your arm out to the side with the ball in it. Bring it back in and show ball on a shit fake, then step in and finish the layup.

3. **Guard Post Spin-Move Drive** With a defender leaning on your back or hip, turn with your dribble -- taking the ball around with you -- and get low to beat the defender. Get to the rim and finish.

4. **High Post Catch, Jab & Turn Jumpshot** Upon receiving the ball, jab your inside foot towards the paint. Then, swing that same leg around you, setting your feet, and firing.

Day 6

1. **Quick-Pivot Right-Hand Hook Shot** Immediately upon catching the ball, plant & turn on your left foot and shoot off the glass with your right hand (switch the foot/hand on the other side).

2. **Shot Fake, One-Dribble Pivot-Spin Move Pullup Jumper** Fake the shot and use a crossover step to attack the middle of the floor. Drop your knee to a 90 degree angle, pivoting and spinning back to the baseline.

3. **High Post Catch, Jab & Turn Jumpshot** Upon receiving the ball, jab your inside foot towards the paint. Then, swing that same leg around you, setting your feet, and firing.

4. **Fade Away / Turn Around Jumpshot** Adjusting your touch is the key to making this shot. Your momentum is going away from the hoop so you must compensate for that. Practice will improve your accuracy.

Day 7

1. **Face-Up Drive, Double Show-Ball Fake, Finish** Attack off the dribble and extend your arm out to the side with the ball in it. Bring it back in and show ball on a shit fake, then step in and finish the layup.

2. **Mid-Post Stepback Jumpshot** Face up to the defense, and use a jab step as you dribble, right into a jumper.

3. **Reverse Pivot Move Layup** Maintaining your pivot foot is key here. With your back turned, swing your baseline-side leg to the middle and fake the shot. Swing that same leg back behind you, jumping and turning to adjust in the air, finishing with a layup.

4. **Baseline Fadeaway Jumper Counter Move - Pivot-Spin Move Finish** Work on both options for the specified reps, each. After showing you can make the fadeaway jumper, use that threat to explode to the rim.

WORKOUT TRACKER: 365 DAYS

Digital Version: HoopHandbook.com/Charts

Date	Workout Series #	Day #	Total Makes	Self-Rating (/100)	Notes

Date	Workout Series #	Day #	Total Makes	Self-Rating (/100)	Notes

Date	Workout Series #	Day #	Total Makes	Self-Rating (/100)	Notes

Date	Workout Series #	Day #	Total Makes	Self-Rating (/100)	Notes

Date	Workout Series #	Day #	Total Makes	Self-Rating (/100)	Notes

Date	Workout Series #	Day #	Total Makes	Self-Rating (/100)	Notes

Date	Workout Series #	Day #	Total Makes	Self-Rating (/100)	Notes

Date	Workout Series #	Day #	Total Makes	Self-Rating (/100)	Notes

Date	Workout Series #	Day #	Total Makes	Self-Rating (/100)	Notes

Date	Workout Series #	Day #	Total Makes	Self-Rating (/100)	Notes

Date	Workout Series #	Day #	Total Makes	Self-Rating (/100)	Notes

Date	Workout Series #	Day #	Total Makes	Self-Rating (/100)	Notes

Date	Workout Series #	Day #	Total Makes	Self-Rating (/100)	Notes

Date	Workout Series #	Day #	Total Makes	Self-Rating (/100)	Notes

Date	Workout Series #	Day #	Total Makes	Self-Rating (/100)	Notes

Date	Workout Series #	Day #	Total Makes	Self-Rating (/100)	Notes

Date	Workout Series #	Day #	Total Makes	Self-Rating (/100)	Notes

Date	Workout Series #	Day #	Total Makes	Self-Rating (/100)	Notes

Date	Workout Series #	Day #	Total Makes	Self-Rating (/100)	Notes

Date	Workout Series #	Day #	Total Makes	Self-Rating (/100)	Notes

Date	Workout Series #	Day #	Total Makes	Self-Rating (/100)	Notes

Date	Workout Series #	Day #	Total Makes	Self-Rating (/100)	Notes

Date	Workout Series #	Day #	Total Makes	Self-Rating (/100)	Notes

Date	Workout Series #	Day #	Total Makes	Self-Rating (/100)	Notes

Date	Workout Series #	Day #	Total Makes	Self-Rating (/100)	Notes

Date	Workout Series #	Day #	Total Makes	Self-Rating (/100)	Notes

Date	Workout Series #	Day #	Total Makes	Self-Rating (/100)	Notes

Date	Workout Series #	Day #	Total Makes	Self-Rating (/100)	Notes

Date	Workout Series #	Day #	Total Makes	Self-Rating (/100)	Notes

ABOUT DRE BALDWIN

Dre Baldwin is the world's only expert on Mental Toughness, Confidence and Self-Discipline. A 9-year professional basketball player, Dre works with athletes, entrepreneurs and business professionals as a speaker, consultant, author and content über-producer.

Dre has worked with Nike, Finish Line, Wendy's Gatorade, Buick, Wilson Sports and DIME magazine.

Dre has been blogging since 2005 and started publishing to YouTube in 2006. He has over 6,000 videos published, with daily content going out to his 126,000+ subscribers and being viewed over 40 million times. Dre's "Work On Your Game" show on Grant Cardone TV is consistently top-5 in views on the network.

Dre has given 3 TED Talks, published 14 books and has a daily podcast, Work On Your Game with DreAllDay. A Philadelphia native and Penn State alum, Dre lives in Miami.

Learn more about Dre at DreAllDay.com and WorkOnYourGameU.com.

OTHER BOOKS BY DRE BALDWIN

Buy A Game

The Mental Handbook

The Mirror Of Motivation

The Super You

The Overseas Basketball Blueprint

Dre Philosophy Vol. 0

The Insta-Philosopher

100 Mental Game Best Practices

25 Conversation Starters

25 Reasons to Quit Worrying

55 Daily People Skills

Ask Yourself A Better Question

The Seller's Mindset

The Mental Workbook

OTHER HOOPHANDBOOK PROGRAMS

The Signature Manuals: Point Guards

The Signature Manuals: Wings

The Signature Manuals: Bigs

The Ultimate Athlete

Position of Power

HoopHandbook: Post Play

HoopHandbook: Ball Handling & Weak Hand

HoopHandbook: Crossover Scoring Moves

HoopHandbook: Scoring Moves

HoopHandbook: Undersized Players

HoopHandbook: Shooting & Shooter Scoring Moves

HoopHandbook: Warm-Up, Defense, Passing & Finishing

HoopHandbook: Vertical & Dunking

HoopHandbook: Triple Threat, 2-Dribble & Jumpstop Moves

HoopHandbook: Beginners & Weekend Warriors

Learn More at HoopHandbook.com

#WOYG

Made in the USA
Coppell, TX
03 December 2022